THIS LAND CALLED AMERICA: MAINE

CREATIVE EDUCATION

Published by Creative Education
P.O. Box 227, Mankato, Minnesota 56002
Creative Education is an imprint of The Creative Company
www.thecreativecompany.us

Book and cover design by Blue Design (www.bluedes.com)
Art direction by Rita Marshall
Printed in the United States of America

Photographs by Alamy (Claudia Adams, Todd Bannor, Bill Brooks,
Donald Enright, Andre Jenny), Corbis (Bettmann, W. Cody, Bob Krist,
Lake County Museum, Hubert Stadler, Underwood & Underwood),
Getty Images (Jose Azel/Aurora, Eddie Brady, Chad Ehlers, Hulton
Archive, Kean Collection, MPI, Robert C. Nunnington, Joe Raedle, Ted
Thai/Time & Life Pictures, Lawrence Thornton, Time Life Pictures/Pix
Inc./Time Life Pictures)

Library of Congress Cataloging-in-Publication Data
Peterson, Sheryl.
Maine / by Sheryl Peterson.
p. cm. — (This land called America)
Includes bibliographical references and index.
ISBN 978-1-58341-644-0
1. Maine—Juvenile literature. I. Title. II. Series.
F19.3.P48 2008
974.1—dc22   2007005709

First Edition
9 8 7 6 5 4 3 2 1

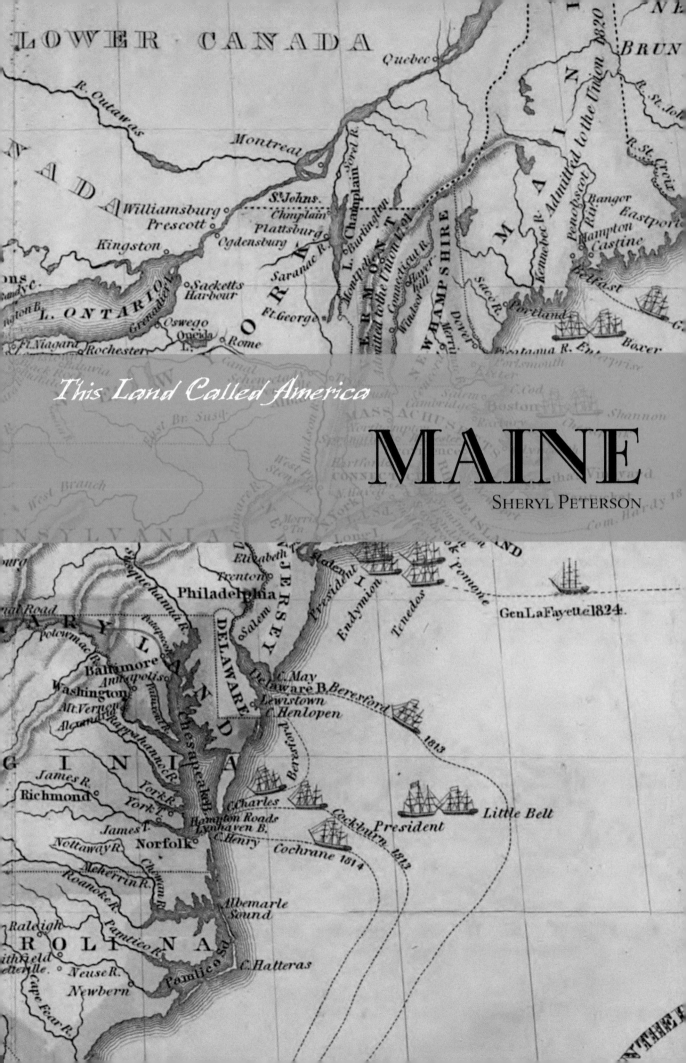

This Land Called America

MAINE

Sheryl Peterson

Maine

SHERYL PETERSON

SALTY SEA SPRAY FILLS THE AIR. SEA GULLS
SHRIEK ALONG THE ROCKY SHORES. OUT ON THE
ATLANTIC OCEAN, LOBSTER CREWS ARE READY TO
START FISHING. FIRST, THEY BAIT THE TRAPS WITH
CHUNKS OF MEAT OR FISH TO ATTRACT THE TASTY
LOBSTERS. THEN THEY LOWER THEIR TRAPS TO
THE OCEAN FLOOR. LOBSTER TRAPS ARE MARKED
WITH COLORED BUOYS. LATER IN THE DAY,
FISHERMEN RETURN TO THE BUOYS AND HOIST UP
THEIR TRAPS. THEY MOTOR BACK TO THE DOCKS
AND UNLOAD THE FRESH, COLD-WATER CATCH
OF THE DAY. FINALLY, SWEET MAINE LOBSTERS
ARE BOILED, DIPPED IN BUTTER, AND SERVED ON
TABLES ACROSS AMERICA.

YEAR

1524 Italian Giovanni da Verrazano becomes the first European to explore the coast of Maine.

EVENT

Maine's Fight for Freedom

SEVERAL AMERICAN INDIAN TRIBES ONCE LIVED IN MAINE. TWO OF THEM WERE THE PENOBSCOT AND THE PASSAMAQUODDY. AROUND 1524, FRENCH EXPLORERS CAME ACROSS THE OCEAN TO MAINE. THEY SAW THAT MAINE WAS A HEAVILY FORESTED LAND WITH MANY FUR-BEARING ANIMALS AND FISH. THE FRENCH CLAIMED THE

SIR Wᴹ PEPPERELL.

SIR J. AMHERST.   GENˡ BRADDOCK.   GENˡ ABERCROMBIE.

GENˡ WOLFE.

The French and Indian War of 1754–1763 (opposite) pitted the French against the English (above), but England's triumph would soon be overturned by the American colonists.

land and called it Acadia. This was a name for parts of Canada and Maine. The French set up trading posts to buy and sell furs throughout Acadia.

In the 1620s, settlers came from England. They claimed Maine for England. Maine became part of the colony of Massachusetts. Settlements were built up, but not many people survived. The land was too rugged, and the climate was too chilly and unpredictable. Local Indian attacks wiped out most of the ill-prepared settlers.

YEAR

1604   French explorer Samuel de Champlain discovers Mount Desert, Maine's largest island.

EVENT

VIEW OF THE CAPITOL, AT AUGUSTA. MAINE.

From 1754 to 1763, the French and English fought over the American territories in a conflict called the French and Indian War. The Indians sided with the French, but the English won. England took control of Maine again until the Revolutionary War began in 1775. The American colonies won that war over England, but Maine suffered many losses. About 4,000 men from Maine lost their lives.

Maine became part of the new United States, but it was also still part of Massachusetts. Soon, many people built homes and churches in Maine. Since the region had plenty of trees for wood, they started lumber businesses.

Then another war with England called the War of 1812 started. When the U.S. won the war, Maine asked to be set apart. In 1820, Maine became the 23rd state in the nation. Augusta was named its capital in 1827. William King, a ship-builder, was sworn in as Maine's first governor.

By this time, the state had more than 300,000 residents, 9 counties, and 236 towns. People came to mine for granite and limestone. They came to fish and to log the forests. Some came to cut ice and sell it to places farther south. Others built railroads.

Augusta was chosen as the best location for the state's grand capitol, which was completed in 1832.

The railroads carried potatoes, Maine's biggest crop, to markets across the state. Workers constructed sawmills along Maine's important rivers. Soon, factories sprang up nearby.

YEAR

1691   Maine becomes the District of Maine under the control of the Massachusetts colony.

EVENT

Oliver Howard lost an arm in the Civil War, but he continued working for former slaves' rights afterward.

Maine workers produced paper, clothing, and leather products in the factories.

During the Civil War, Maine men served with the Union, or Northern, forces. Maine was a free state and did not want slavery. Oliver Otis Howard and Joshua L. Chamberlain were two successful Union generals from Maine. They were both educated men. Howard later founded Howard University in Washington, D.C. Chamberlain became the president of Bowdoin College in Brunswick.

In 1854, Hannibal Hamlin formed the Republican Party in Maine. He served as Maine's first Republican governor. In 1860, Hamlin was elected to be the first Republican vice president under Abraham Lincoln. The state's Republican Party stayed in power until 1954, when Democrat Edmund Muskie was elected governor. Muskie became a fighter for clean air. In 1968, he was the candidate for vice president with Herbert Humphrey.

In the 20th century, Maine's economy continued to grow and prosper, but it was at a slower pace. The paper industry expanded. Large potato and dairy farms replaced small family farms. Tourism brought in more money to the state.

YEAR

1788   Slavery is outlawed in Maine and Massachusetts.

EVENT

Pine Tree State

MAINE IS THE LARGEST OF THE SIX STATES IN NEW ENGLAND, THE NORTHEASTERN PART OF THE U.S. IT IS THE ONLY STATE IN THE COUNTRY WITH JUST ONE STATE ON ITS BORDER. NEW HAMPSHIRE FORMS MAINE'S WESTERN BORDER. NEW BRUNSWICK, CANADA, IS TO THE NORTHEAST, WHILE QUEBEC, CANADA, LIES TO THE NORTHWEST. MAINE'S SOUTHERN SIDE IS FORMED BY

the Atlantic Ocean, where the state's six largest cities are strung like pearls along the coast.

Rugged mountains cover the northern end of Maine's Atlantic coast. The southern part has sandy beaches. More than 400 islands lie off of Maine's shores. Two of the largest bays are Penobscot and Casco. Inland from the coast is a region known as the Coastal Lowlands. North of the lowlands is the Eastern New England Uplands, an area full of forests and farmland.

The White Mountains tower above northwestern Maine. Mount Katahdin is the highest point at 5,268 feet (1,606 m). In these mountains are hundreds of lakes formed long ago by melted glaciers, or huge sheets of ice. The largest, Moosehead Lake, is shaped like a moose's head, complete with antlers.

Three rivers flow along Maine's border with Canada. They are the St. John, St. Francis, and St. Croix rivers. More than 5,000 other rivers and streams wind through the state of Maine. They all empty into the Atlantic Ocean. Maine has some of the only unspoiled wilderness areas left in the U.S. There is only a handful of towns anywhere near northern Maine's side of the border with Canada.

In Baxter State Park, nature lovers walk the wooded trails (opposite), and some tackle the challenge of hiking on Mount Katahdin (above).

YEAR
1791   Portland Head Light, the oldest lighthouse on the Atlantic, is built on Cape Elizabeth.
EVENT

- 13 -

M

aine has dense forests of Norway pine and white pine, giving it the nickname "The Pine Tree State." Hardwoods such as birch and maple also grow in Maine's wooded regions. At one time, the state was almost stripped of its pines for use in shipbuilding. Now, new trees are constantly planted, sprayed to protect against insects, and watched over by forest rangers.

Where there are trees, there is sure to be wildlife. In Maine, moose feed by the lakeshores. Black bears wander through the mountains. Trout and salmon flip in the rivers and lakes. Seals dip and dive along the coast. Lobsters, which have made

The logging industry takes down many trees in Maine, transporting them on the rivers (above), but some forested areas are left undisturbed (opposite).

1807   Poet Henry Wadsworth Longfellow is born in Portland on February 27.

Early 20th-century postcards liked to exaggerate the extraordinary size of the state's potato crop.

Maine famous, lurk in the coastal waters. Owls, ducks, and eagles all nest in Maine. They fly south to warmer places in the fall.

Every winter, Maine is buried under mounds of snow. Mountain areas can receive more than nine feet (3 m) each winter. The snow is ideal for skiers at Squaw and Sugarloaf mountains. In the fall, strong windstorms called "nor'easters" blow in giant waves along the shoreline.

Potatoes are Maine's most important crop. Aroostook County is famous for its potatoes. Even though most potatoes are now picked by machines, children in northern Maine still have a fall "harvest recess," in which they help with the potato harvest. Teenagers make money by hand-picking the potatoes. Apples, oats, and chickens are other major farm products in Maine.

Maine raises more wild blueberries on its rocky hillsides than any other state. Blueberries are harvested from late July to early September and made into jam and jellies or sold fresh. Maple syrup is another Maine product. In the cold winter months, thousands of maple trees are tapped. The sap is boiled into syrup and shipped all over the U.S.

YEAR

1839   The battle over the Maine-Canada border, known as the "Aroostook War," begins.

EVENT

Creative Mainers

MAINE IS AMERICA'S LEAST-CROWDED EASTERN STATE. MOST RESIDENTS LIVE CLOSE TO THE COAST IN SMALL TOWNS AND ON FARMS. FEW PEOPLE LIVE IN THE NORTH OR WEST. ABOUT ONE-FOURTH OF THE PEOPLE IN MAINE LIVE IN PORTLAND, THE LARGEST CITY IN THE STATE. PEOPLE WHO LIVE IN MAINE ARE CALLED MAINERS.

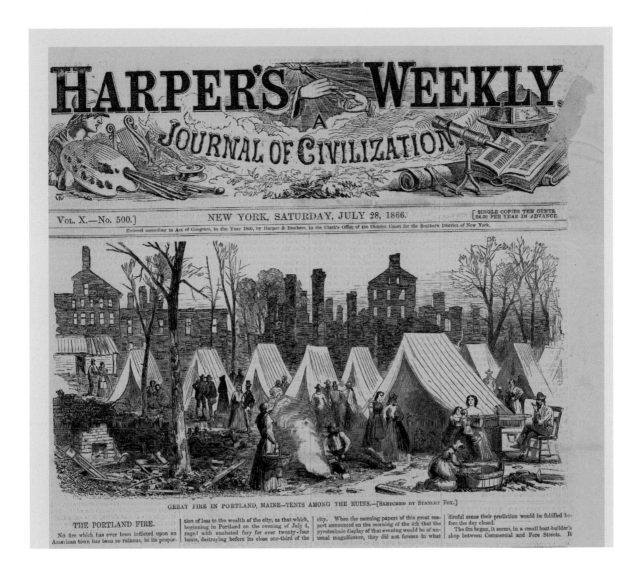

HARPER'S WEEKLY.

JOURNAL OF CIVILIZATION.

VOL. X.—No. 500.]   NEW YORK, SATURDAY, JULY 28, 1866.   [SINGLE COPIES TEN CENTS.
[$4.00 PER YEAR IN ADVANCE.

Entered according to Act of Congress, in the Year 1866, by Harper & Brothers, in the Clerk's Office of the District Court for the Southern District of New York.

GREAT FIRE IN PORTLAND, MAINE—TENTS AMONG THE RUINS.—[Sketched by Stanley Fox.]

THE PORTLAND FIRE.

No fire which has ever been inflicted upon an American town has been so ruinous, in its propor- | tion of loss to the wealth of the city, as that which, beginning in Portland on the evening of July 4, raged with unabated fury for over twenty-four hours, destroying before its close one-third of the | city. When the morning papers of this great sea- port announced on the morning of the 4th that the pyrotechnic display of that evening would be of un- usual magnificence, they did not foresee in what | direful sense their prediction would be fulfilled be- fore the day closed.

The fire began, it seems, in a small boat-builder's shop between Commercial and Fore Streets. It

The Great Fire of Portland left many people homeless in 1866 (above), but the city soon rebuilt itself with sturdy brick buildings (opposite).

Almost all Mainers are white people with European backgrounds. Some Mainers are French Americans. They speak French in their homes and have French newspapers and radio stations. There are still some American Indians in Maine, too. The Penobscot and Passamaquoddy tribes live on reservations. These are areas of land that the U.S. government set aside for American Indians when settlers forced them off their native lands.

Since about 90 percent of Maine is covered with trees, many of Maine's residents work in the logging business. Lumber is the state's leading wood product, but workers also

Paper mills were originally built along rivers to make it easy for logs to be transported to them.

make cardboard boxes, paper bags, and newsprint. There are paper mills in Rumford, Millinocket, and Woodland. There, wood pulp is turned into paper. Maine also produces almost all of the nation's toothpicks.

Maine is home to many creative people. The seacoasts and woods of Maine have inspired many artists and writers. Henry Wadsworth Longfellow, one of America's best-loved poets, was born in Portland in 1807. He called his city "the beautiful town that is seated by the sea." Longfellow is best known for his poem *The Song of Hiawatha*, based on American Indian legends.

E. B. White was also a well-known Maine author. He lived in Maine for 45 years. White wrote the classic children's

When Henry Wadsworth Longfellow was born in Portland, it was still part of Massachusetts.

YEAR

1866 A huge fire on July 4 destroys much of downtown Portland.

EVENT

Mainer Margaret Chase Smith becomes the first woman to serve in both houses of Congress.

Author Stephen King's books had sold more than 100 million copies worldwide by the 1990s.

books *Charlotte's Web, Stuart Little,* and *The Trumpet of the Swan.* Another Maine writer is Stephen King. He was born in Portland and now lives in Bangor. His stories are very different from E. B. White's. King's stories are mostly scary ones, such as *The Shining* and *Pet Sematary*.

People in Maine like to do things for themselves. Some Mainers make their own handcrafted pottery. Clay is shaped by hand into bowls and plates. Then it is fired in a stove called a kiln. The pottery is painted and sold at shops across Maine. For more than 25 years, the Potters Market in Portland has sold pottery from Maine artists. People also take classes from experienced potters. They learn how to form clay on a potter's wheel.

E. B. White was an important writer for a magazine called THE NEW YORKER for almost 50 years.

YEAR

1967   Passamaquoddy and Penobscot Indians are extended the right to vote in state elections.

EVENT

Leon Leonwood, or "L. L.," Bean, was a Mainer who liked to make things by hand. Bean started a mail-order catalog in 1912. He sold boots. Of the first 100 boots sold, 90 were returned. Bean gave back the customers' money and worked harder to make a better boot. Today, the L. L. Bean factory is located in Freeport, Maine. People from all over the U.S. order outdoor gear and clothing from the L. L. Bean catalog.

Mainers like to get involved in politics. Margaret Chase Smith was born in Skowhegan in 1897. She became the first woman to serve in the U.S. House of Representatives. She was also the first woman in the Senate, serving as a senator for 24 years. Smith even ran for president in 1964. People in Maine are independent individuals who like being creative. That is why their state is unique in so many ways.

Margaret Chase Smith (above) helped pave the way for other women to be involved in politics, while L. L. Bean left his company (opposite) a legacy of service and respect.

1980   The U.S. government pays Maine Indian tribes $81.5 million for land illegally taken 200 years earlier.

Beside the Sea

WHEN MANY PEOPLE THINK OF MAINE, THEY THINK OF LOBSTERS. PEOPLE HAVE BEEN FISHING IN THE WATERS OFF MAINE'S COAST FOR HUNDREDS OF YEARS. TODAY, HUNDREDS OF LOBSTER FISHING BOATS PATROL THE AREA. MAINE PRODUCES ALMOST ALL OF THE NATION'S LOBSTER. THESE TOUGH-LOOKING SHELLFISH THRIVE IN THE CLEAN COASTAL WATERS.

Many people think Maine cold-water lobsters are some of the world's most delicious foods. But they don't realize the hard work it takes to catch them. Maine trap-tenders go out to sea in all but the most extreme weather. Lobster boats today are equipped with modern high-tech gear, but the lobster is harvested the same way it has been for hundreds of years.

Tourists travel to Maine to eat fresh lobster. The state's restaurants are famous for their live lobsters. Herring, Atlantic salmon, and scallops are also caught in Maine's ocean water. Some people dig up clams, too. Every day, Maine seafood is enjoyed around the country.

There is more than lobster boats to see along Maine's shores. The state's rocky coastline has about 60 lighthouses that once guided ships at sea to safety. The oldest and most famous lighthouse in Maine is the Portland Head Light on Cape Elizabeth. President George Washington ordered the lighthouse to be built in 1791. The lighthouse keeper's house has since been made into a museum.

Up the Maine coast from Portland Head Light (opposite) is the town of Trenton, famous for its fresh lobster-shipping business (above).

Pemaquid Point Lighthouse has a white, cone-shaped tower. It is in an area of smooth sandy beaches. West Quoddy Head Light has candy-cane red and white stripes. Its beacon flashes from the coastal point that lies farthest east in the nation. Maine lighthouses are popular tourist attractions.

Many Mainers enjoy sailing. They even build their own wooden boats. There is a boat-building school in Brooklin, Maine. A team of workers can build a sturdy cedar boat in six days there. Maine residents celebrate Windjammer Days in July. Windjammers are large ships with two sails. People take relaxing windjammer cruises out of Rockland and Camden's harbors.

People in Maine love sports. The University of Maine's men's and women's teams are called the Black Bears. Basket-

People in Maine enjoy building boats by hand (opposite) and visiting the smooth rocks of Acadia National Park (above) on Mount Desert Island.

YEAR
1996   Nineteen inches (48 cm) of rain falls in 48 hours in the Camp Ellis area, causing major flooding.
EVENT

Senator William Cohen from Bangor is sworn in as President Bill Clinton's secretary of defense.

QUICK FACTS

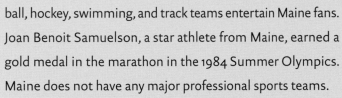

Population: 1,321,574

Largest City: Portland (pop. 63,635)

Capital: Augusta

Entered the union: March 15, 1820

Nickname: Pine Tree State, Vacationland

State flower: white pine cone and tassel

State bird: black-capped chickadee

Size: 35,385 sq mi (91,647 sq km)—39th-biggest in U.S.

Major industries: fishing, lobster trapping, paper making, tourism

ball, hockey, swimming, and track teams entertain Maine fans. Joan Benoit Samuelson, a star athlete from Maine, earned a gold medal in the marathon in the 1984 Summer Olympics. Maine does not have any major professional sports teams.

Acadia National Park is a popular place to explore nature. Acadia is east of Penobscot Bay on Mount Desert Island. It is the only national park in New England. Acadia Park has mountains and forests. It also has lakes, ocean views, and islands. Thunderhole is a beach in the park. It is named after the loud, crashing surf.

Acadia is also home to Cadillac Mountain. At 1,532 feet (467 m) tall, it is the highest point on the Atlantic seaboard north of Brazil, a country in South America. People come to the park to hike the granite peaks, bike on historic carriage roads, and simply enjoy the scenery.

People in Maine love the variety their state has to offer. There are tall mountains and thick forests, clear lakes and a rugged ocean coast. Maine is a place to enjoy the outdoors and a place to be creative and make things by hand. Maine is a state with fresh crisp air, four distinct seasons, and endless opportunities for all its residents.

YEAR
2006 John E. Baldacci is re-elected governor of Maine.
EVENT

BIBLIOGRAPHY

Hamlin, Helen, and Dean Bennett. *Nine Mile Bridge: Three Years in the Maine Woods*. Yarmouth, Maine: Islandport Press, 2007.

Kent, Deborah. *Maine*. New York: Children's Press, 1999.

Kummer, Patricia. *Maine*. Mankato, Minn.: Bridgestone Books, 1998.

Lester, S. Terrell, et al. *Maine: The Seasons*. New York: Knopf, 2001.

McCauley, Brian, and Matthew Dimock. *The Names of Maine*. Bar Harbor, Maine: Acadia Press, 2005.

State of Maine. "Maine Facts and History." Official Web Site of the State of Maine. http://www.maine.gov/portal/facts_history/.

INDEX